RECORDED VERSIONS
GUITAR ®

AUTHENTIC TRANSCRIPTIONS
WITH NOTES AND TABLATURE

THE OFFSPRING

AMERICANA

www.offspring.com

ALL SONGS BY DEXTER HOLLAND, EXCEPT
"FEELINGS" BY MORRIS ALBERT AND
LOUIS GASTE, WITH LYRICAL PARODY BY DEXTER HOLLAND.

MUSIC TRANSCRIPTIONS BY JEFF JACOBSON, STEVE GORENBERG,
AND PETE BILLMANN

ALL PHOTOGRAPHY BY F. SCOTT SCHAFER EXCEPT PAGE 8
BY JAY BLAKESBURG

ISBN 0-634-00632-0

HAL•LEONARD®
CORPORATION

7777 W. BLUEMOUND RD. P.O. BOX 13819 MILWAUKEE, WI 53213

Visit Hal Leonard Online at **www.halleonard.com**

THE OFFSPRING

AMERICANA

CONTENTS

Have You Ever

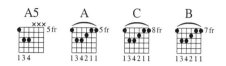

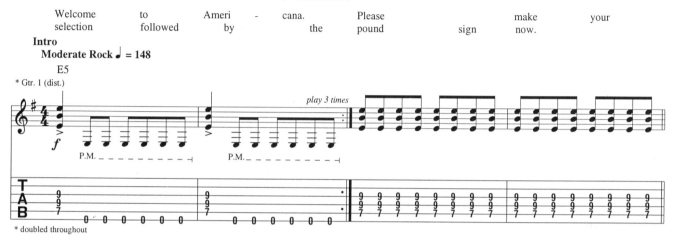

Welcome

Welcome to Ameri - cana. Please make your
selection followed by the pound sign now.

*Gtr. 1: w/ Rhy. Fig. 2, 2 times

E5   C5   G5   D5

Some days my soul's __ con - fined __ and out of mind, _ sleep __ for - ev - er.

Voc. Fig. 1   End Voc. Fig. 1

Fall - ing. I'm fall - ing.

Rhy. Fig. 3   End Rhy. Fig. 3

Gtr. 2

pp fade in*

Gradually fade out.

Voc.: w/ Voc. Fig. 1, 3 times
Gtr. 2: w/ Rhy. Fig. 3, 3 times

E5   C5   G5

Some days my dark - est friend __ is me a - gain. __ Have __

D5   Gtr. 1 tacet
                   N.C.(E5)
                   *

__ you ev - er? Some - day I'll try __ a - gain __ and

All voices gradually fade out.

not pre - tend, __ this time __ for - ev - er. Some - day I'll get __

End Double-Time Feel

__ it straight, _ but not to - day. __ Have __ you ev - er?

Interlude

E5

Gtr. 2

dim.   (cont. in slash)

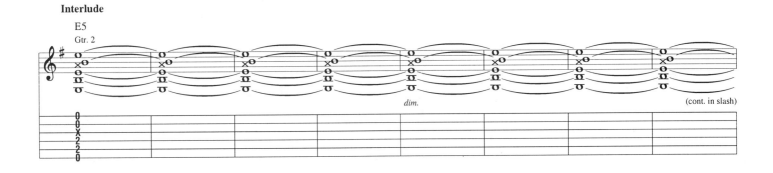

Segue to "Staring at the Sun"

Additional Lyrics

2. Someday I'll try again and not pretend,
   This time forever.
   Someday I'll get it straight, but not today.
   Have you ever?

Staring At the Sun

D5

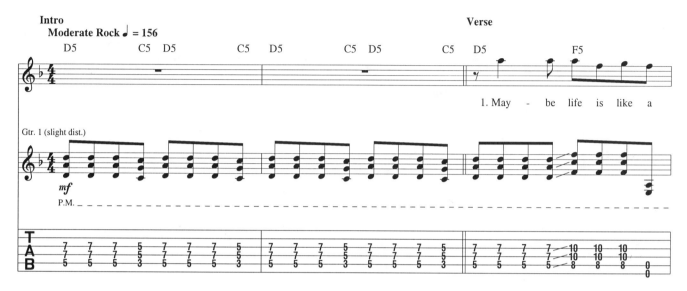

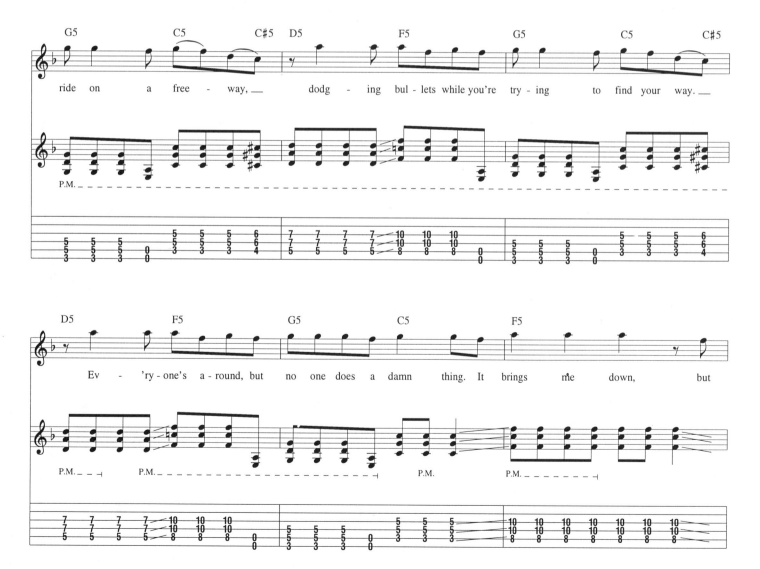

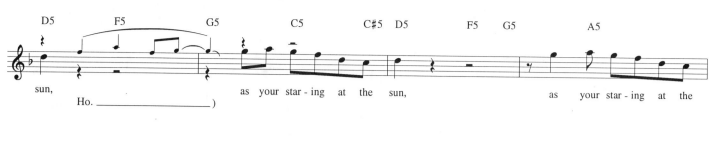

sun,
Ho. _____)
as your star - ing at the sun,
as your star - ing at the

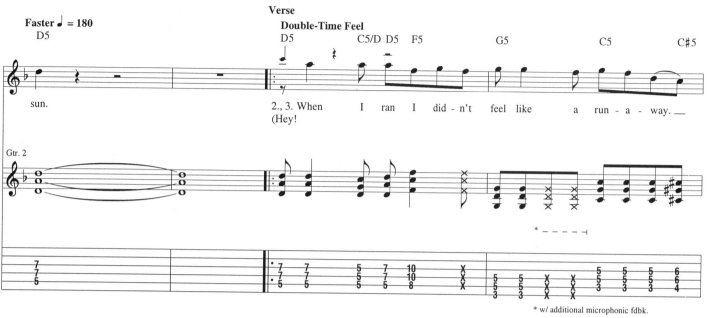

Faster ♩ = 180

Verse
Double-Time Feel

sun.
2., 3. When I ran I did - n't feel like a run - a - way. __
(Hey!

Gtr. 2

* w/ additional microphonic fdbk.

When I es - caped I did - n't feel like I got a - way. __ There's more to liv - ing than a
Hey!
Hey!)

Harm. ⌐

on - ly sur - viv - ing. May - be I'm not there, but I'm still try - ing. Though you

Harm. ⌐

Pretty Fly (For a White Guy)

The Kids Aren't Alright

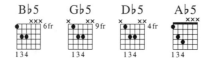

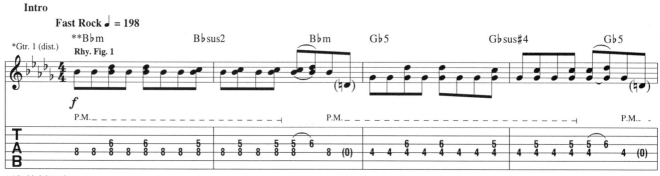

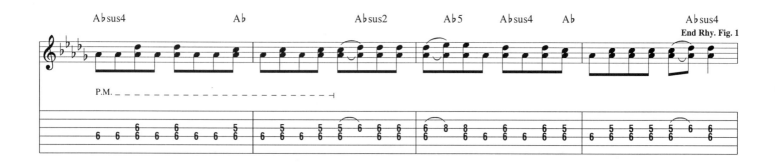

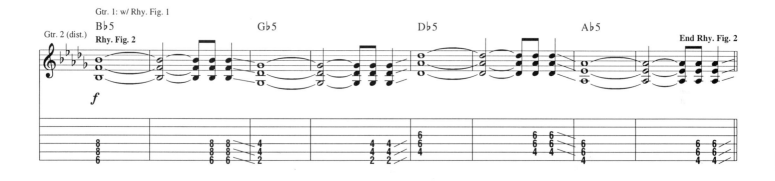

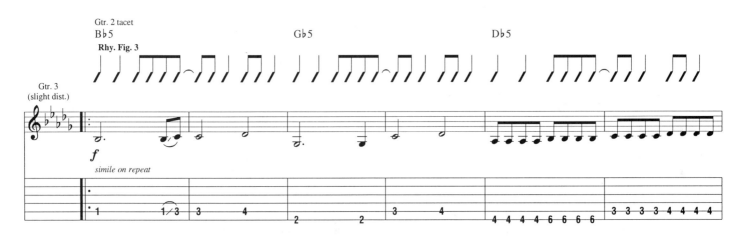

1. When we were young the fu-ture was so bright, __ the old neigh-bor-hood was so a - live. __ Whoa. ___

2. See Additional Lyrics

And ev-'ry kid on the whole damn street __ was gon-na make it big and not be beat. __ Whoa. __

Now the neigh-bor-hood's cracked and torn, __ the kids are grown up but their lives are worn. __
Whoa. __   Whoa. __

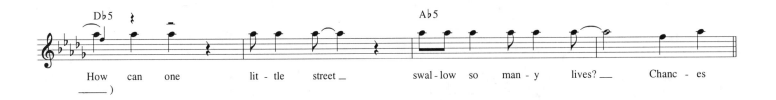

How can one lit-tle street __ swal-low so man-y lives? __ Chanc - es
__)

Chorus

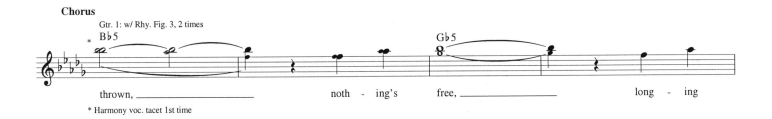

thrown, _____ noth - ing's free, _____ long - ing

* Harmony voc. tacet 1st time

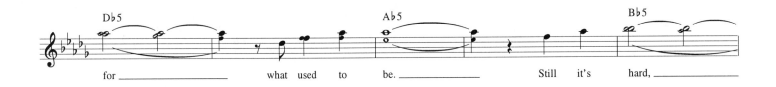

for _____ what used to be. _____ Still it's hard, _____

__ hard to see. _____ Frag - ile lives, _____ shat - tered

Guitar Solo

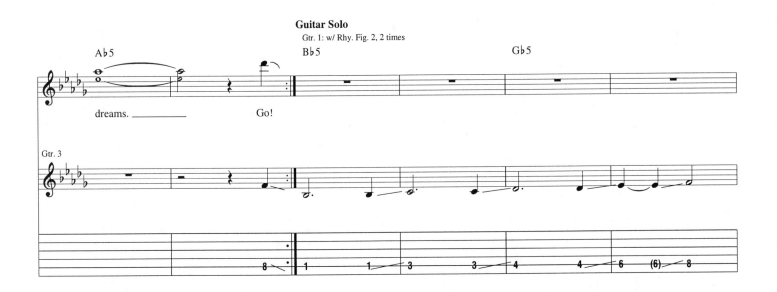

dreams. _____ Go!

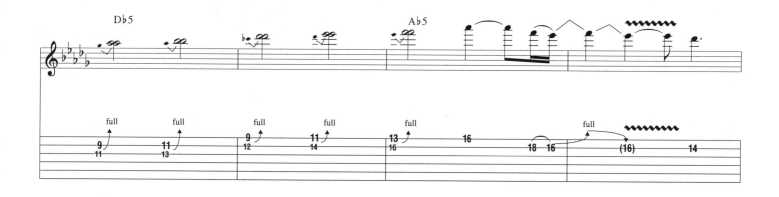

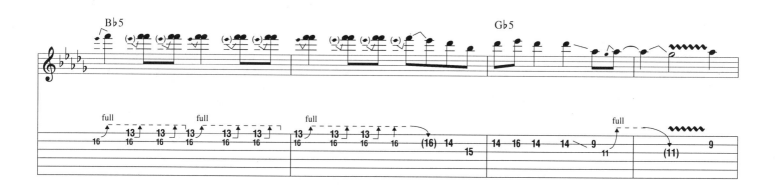

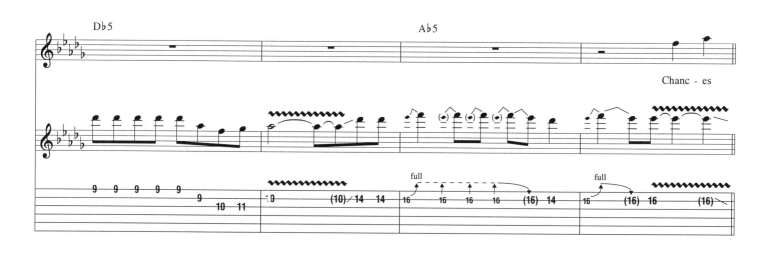

Chanc - es

Chorus

Gtr. 1: w/ Rhy. Fig. 3, 2 times

Gtr. 3 tacet

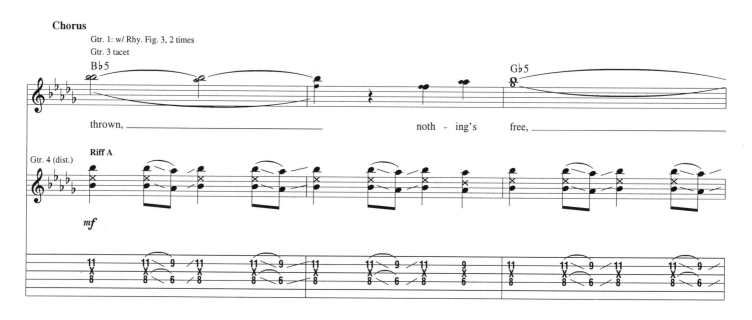

thrown, _____ noth - ing's free, _____

Gtr. 4 (dist.)

Riff A

mf

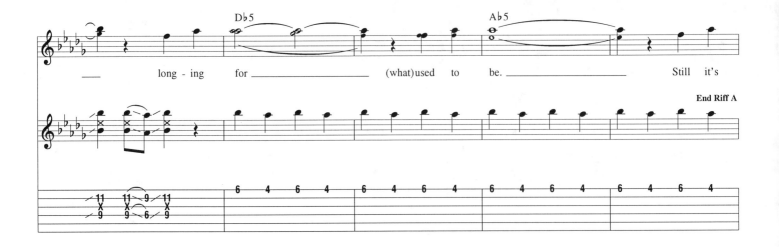

long - ing for _____ (what)used to be. _____ Still it's

End Riff A

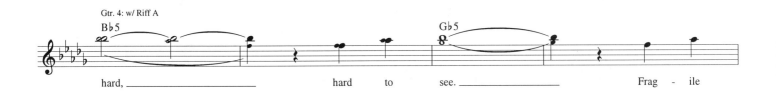

Gtr. 4: w/ Riff A

hard, _____ hard to see. _____ Frag - ile

lives, _____ shat - tered dreams. _____

Bb5

Gtr. 4

Gtr. 1
divisi

Additional Lyrics

2. Jamie had a chance, well, she really did;
   Instead she dropped out and had a couple of kids.
   Mark still lives at home 'cause he's got no job;
   He just plays guitar and smokes a lot of pot.
   Jay committed suicide,
   Brandon O.D.'d and died.
   What the hell is going on?
   The cruellest dream, reality.

Feelings

Words and Music by Morris Albert and Louis Gaste
with lyrical parody by Dexter Holland

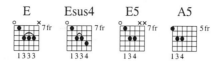

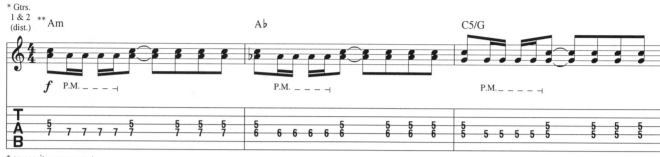

Intro
Fast Rock ♩ = 184
Double-Time Feel

* composite arrangement
** Chord symbols reflect implied tonality.

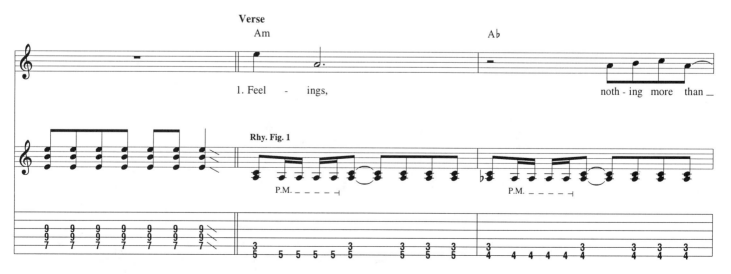

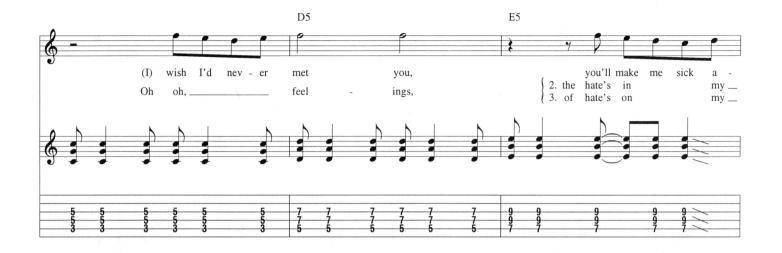

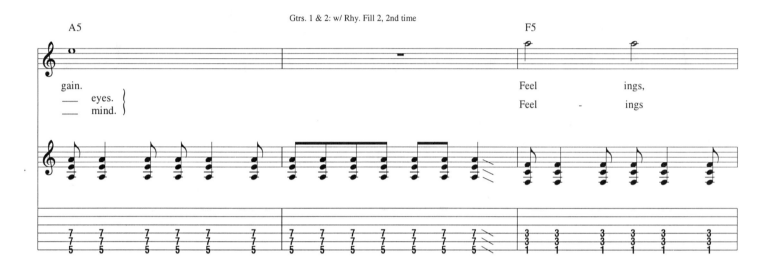

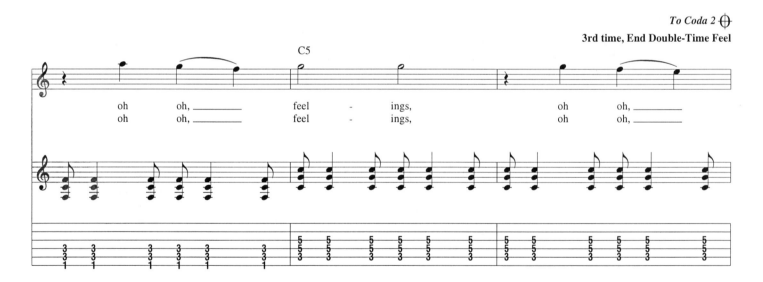

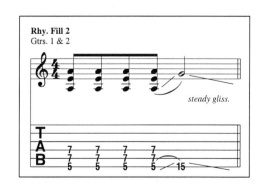

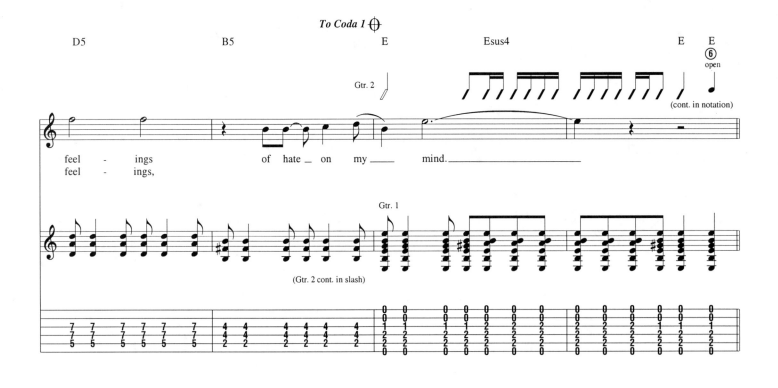

To Coda 1

feel - ings of hate — on my ___ mind. ___

feel - ings,

Verse

Gtrs. 1 & 2: w/ Rhy. Fif. 1, 2 times

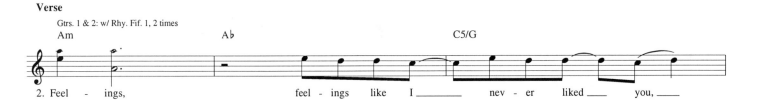

2. Feel - ings, feel - ings like I ___ nev - er liked ___ you, ___

feel - ings like I ___ wan - na kill ___ you. ___ Live in my ___

___ heart. feel - ings, feel - ings like I ___

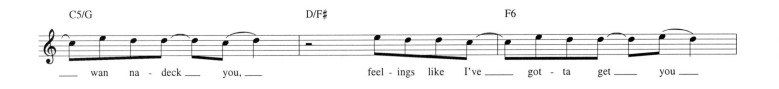

___ wan - na deck ___ you, ___ feel - ings like I've ___ got - ta get ___ you ___

D.S. al Coda 1

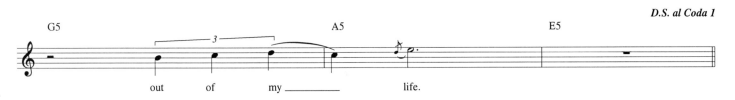

out of my ___ life.

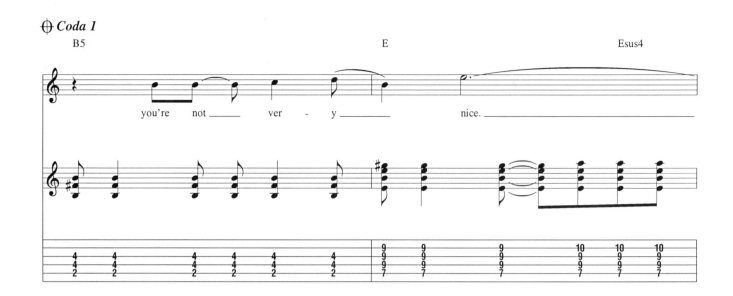

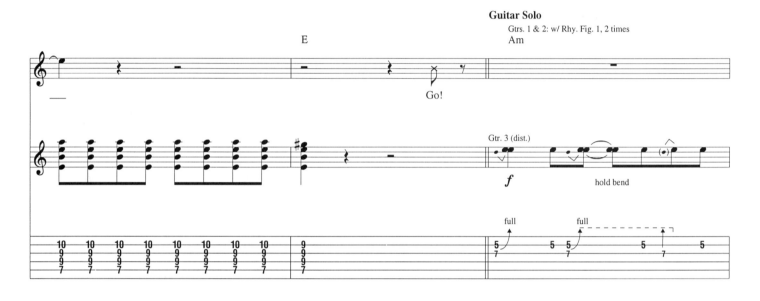

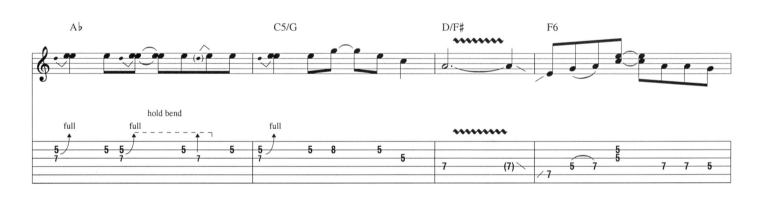

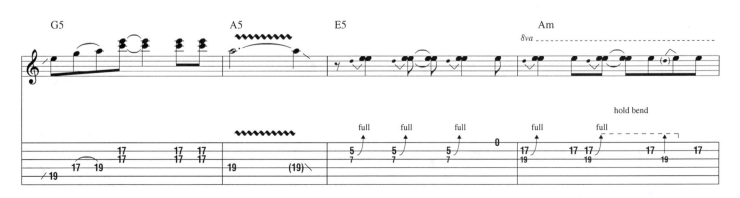

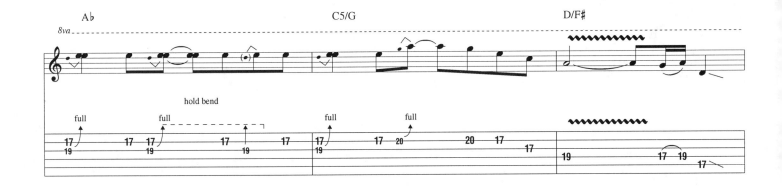

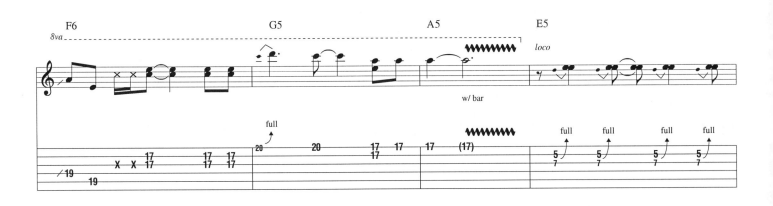

D.S. al Coda 2

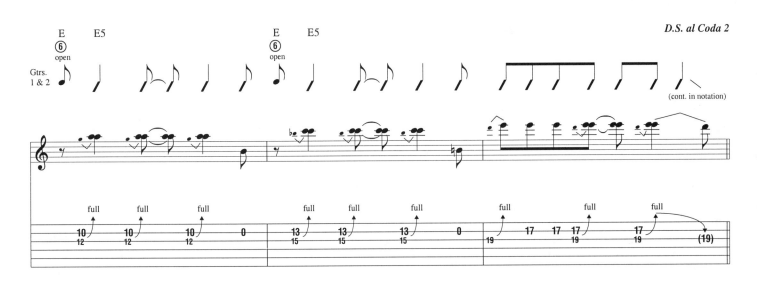

She's Got Issues

Intro

Moderate Rock ♩ = 123

*Gtr. 1 (dist.)

f

**P.M.

*doubled throughout

**Gradually release P.M.

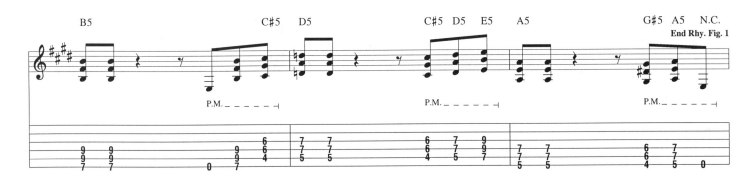

P.M.

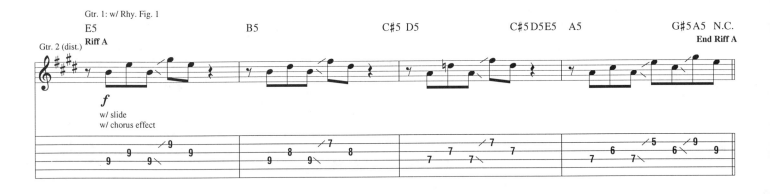

Gtr. 1: w/ Rhy. Fig. 1

Gtr. 2 (dist.)

Riff A

f

w/ slide
w/ chorus effect

End Riff A

Verse

Gtr. 2 tacet

Gtr. 1 tacet

1. I'm see- ing this girl and she ___ just _____ might be out of her mind. ___

Gtr. 1

Rhy. Fill 1

End Rhy. Fill 1

*Chord symbols reflect implied tonality.

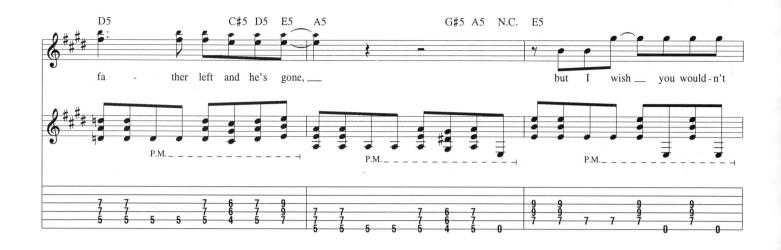

fa - ther left and he's gone, ___ but I wish ___ you would - n't

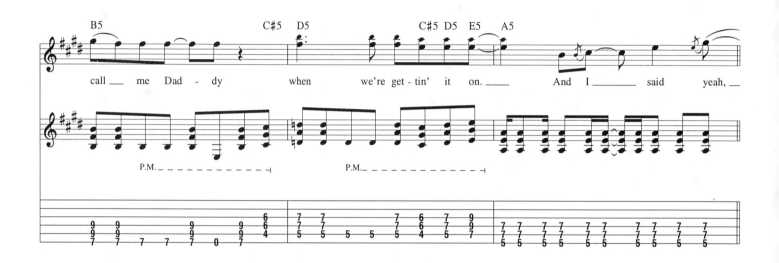

call ___ me Dad - dy when we're get - tin' it on. ___ And I ___ said yeah, ___

Chorus

Gtr. 1: w/ Rhy. Fig. 3, 4 times

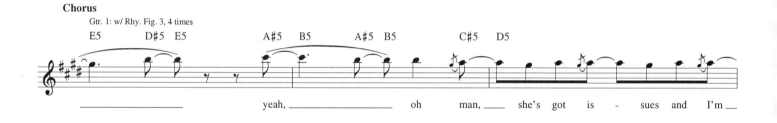

_____ yeah, _____ oh man, ___ she's got is - sues and I'm ___

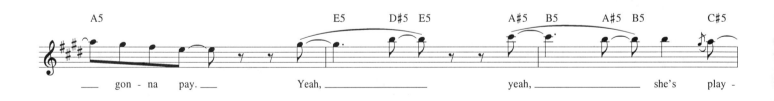

___ gon - na pay. ___ Yeah, _____ yeah, _____ she's play -

Gtr. 2: w/ Riff A, 2 times

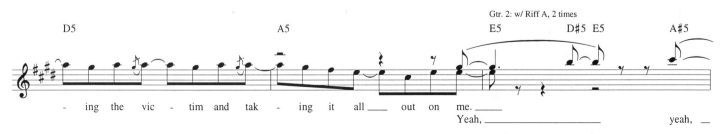

- ing the vic - tim and tak - ing it all ___ out on me. ___

Yeah, _____ yeah, ___

my god, ___ she's got is - sues and I'm ___ gon - na pay, _ gon - na pay, _

_ gon - na pay, _ gon - na pay, _ gon - na pay, _ gon - na pay, ___ woo! _ Wow! _____

Outro

Bkgd. Voc.: w/ Voc. Fig. 1, 3 1/2 times
Gtr. 1: w/ Rhy. Fig. 4, 3 1/2 times

If you think I'm con - trol - ling, then why do you fol -

- low me a - round? _ If you're not co - de - pend - ent,

then why do you let oth - ers drag _ you _ down? _ I don't know why you're messed _ up.

I don't know why your whole _ life is ___ a ___ chore. _ Just do me a fa - vor,

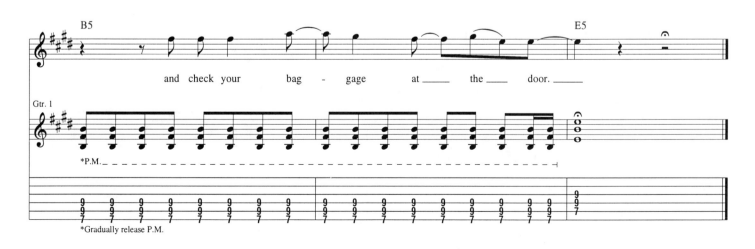

and check your bag - gage at ___ the ___ door. ____

Gtr. 1

*P.M. ‑ ‑ ‑ ‑ ‑ ‑ ‑ ‑ ‑ ‑ ‑ ‑ ‑ ‑ ‑ ‑

*Gradually release P.M.

Walla Walla

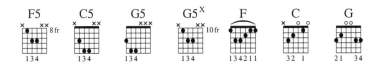

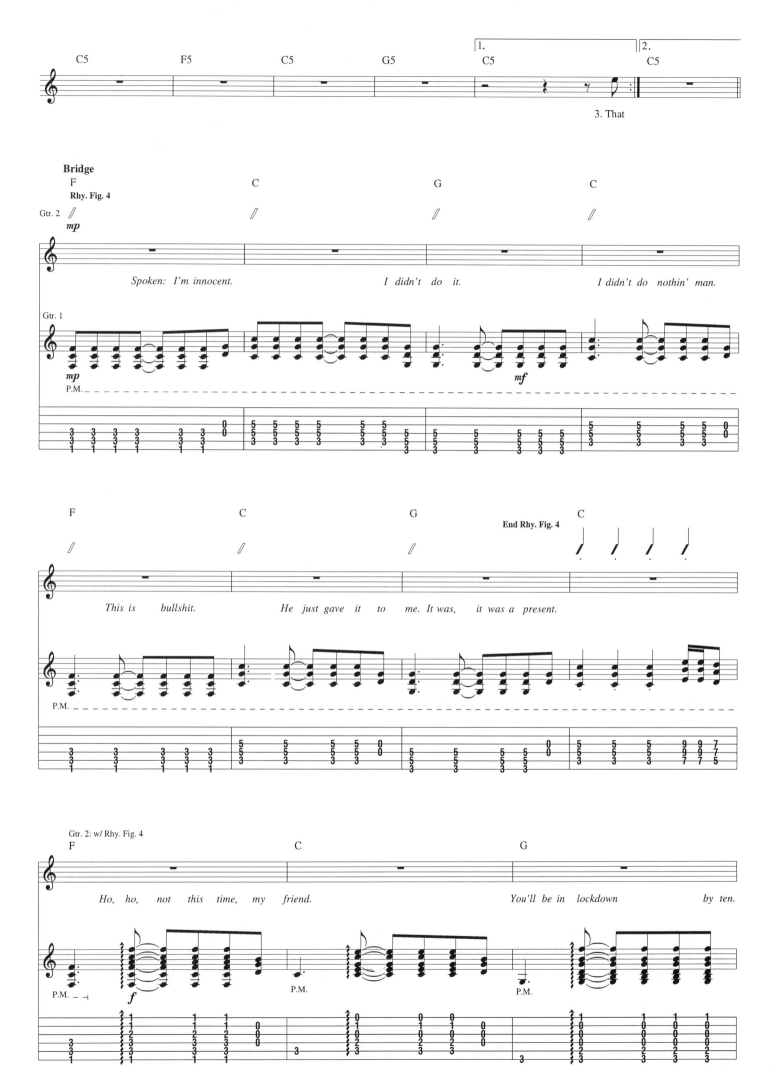

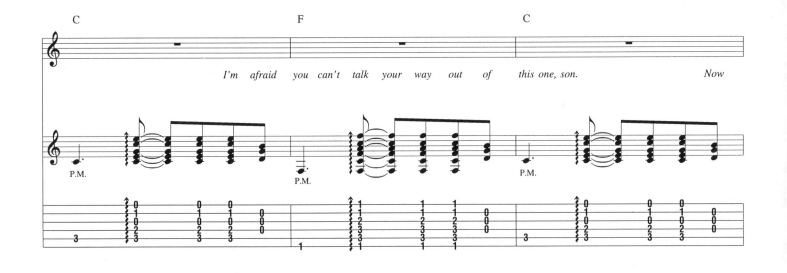

I'm afraid you can't talk your way out of this one, son. Now

D.S. al Coda

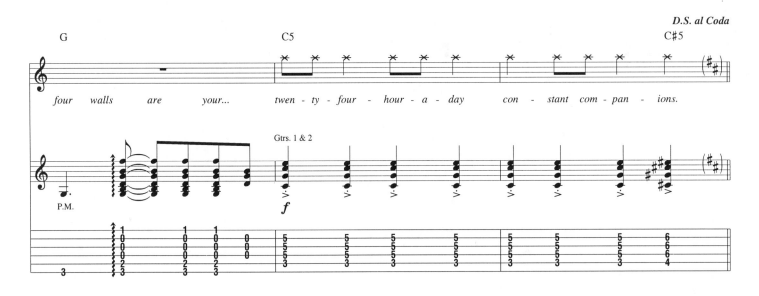

four walls are your... twen-ty-four-hour-a-day con-stant com-pan-ions.

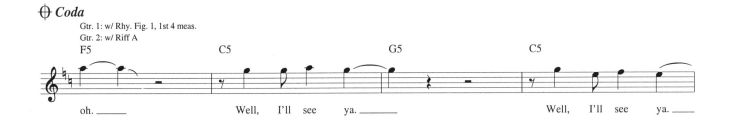

Coda

Gtr. 1: w/ Rhy. Fig. 1, 1st 4 meas.
Gtr. 2: w/ Riff A

oh. _____ Well, I'll see ya. _____ Well, I'll see ya. _____

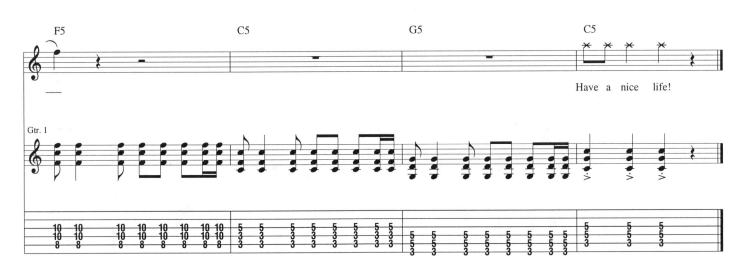

_____ Have a nice life!

Gtr. 1

The End of the Line

Interlude
F#5

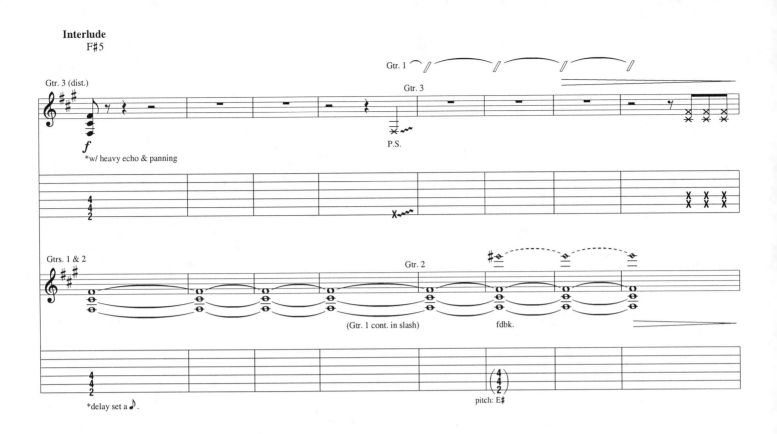

*w/ heavy echo & panning

P.S.

(Gtr. 1 cont. in slash)   fdbk.

pitch: E#

*delay set a ♪.

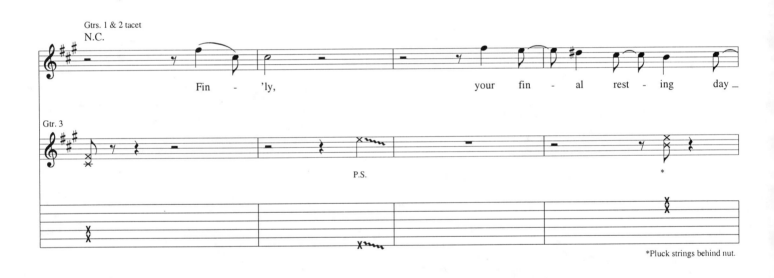

Gtrs. 1 & 2 tacet
N.C.

Fin - 'ly,   your fin - al rest - ing day

P.S.

*Pluck strings behind nut.

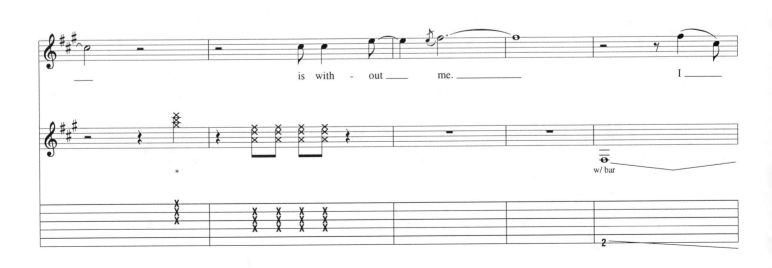

is with - out ___ me. ___   I ___

w/ bar

50

No Brakes

Why Don't You Get a Job?

Chorus

Gtr. 1: w/ Rhy. Fig. 1, last 4 meas., 2 times

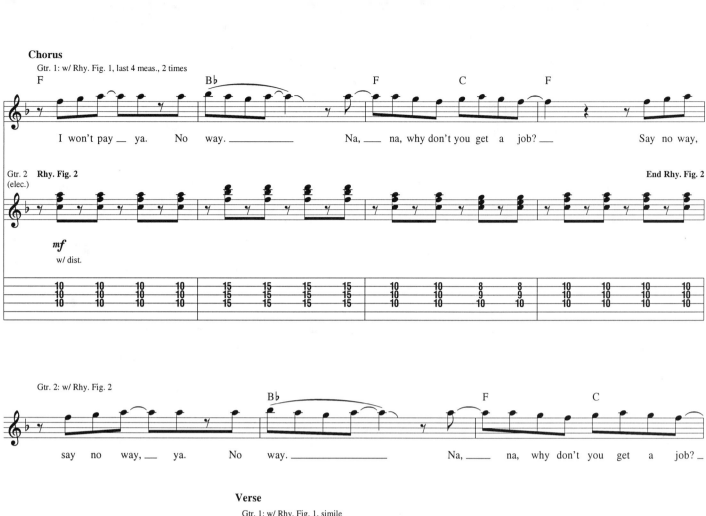

I won't pay ___ ya. No way. ___ Na, ___ na, why don't you get a job? ___ Say no way,

Gtr. 2   **Rhy. Fig. 2**
(elec.)

mf
w/ dist.

End Rhy. Fig. 2

Gtr. 2: w/ Rhy. Fig. 2

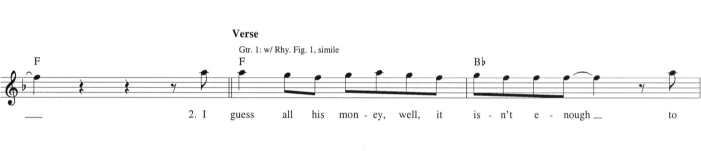

say no way, ___ ya. No way. ___ Na, ___ na, why don't you get a job? ___

Verse

Gtr. 1: w/ Rhy. Fig. 1, simile

2. I guess all his mon-ey, well, it is-n't e-nough ___ to

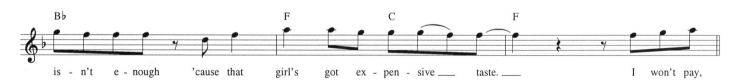

keep her bill col-lec-tors at bay. ___ I guess all his mon-ey, well, it

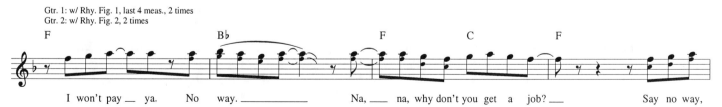

is-n't e-nough 'cause that girl's got ex-pen-sive ___ taste. ___ I won't pay,

Chorus

Gtr. 1: w/ Rhy. Fig. 1, last 4 meas., 2 times
Gtr. 2: w/ Rhy. Fig. 2, 2 times

I won't pay ___ ya. No way. ___ Na, ___ na, why don't you get a job? ___ Say no way,

say no way, ___ ya. No way. ___ Na, ___ na, why don't you get a job? ___

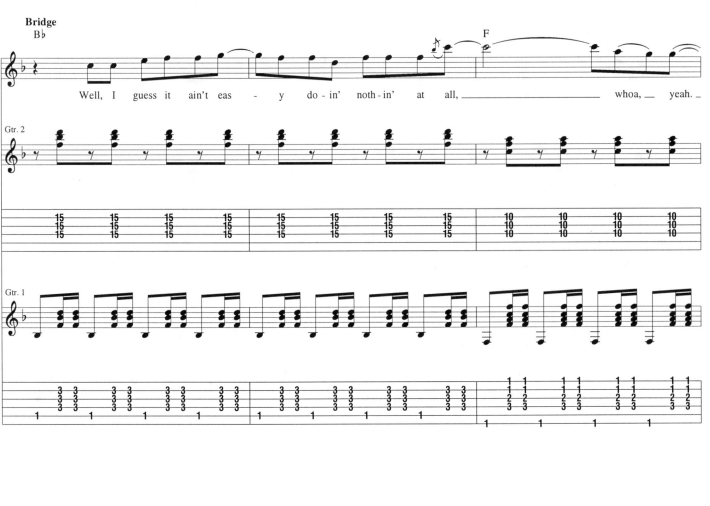

___ na, why don't you get a job? ___ Say no way, say no way, ___ ya. No

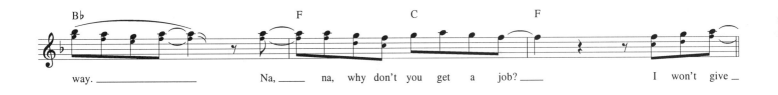

way. _____ Na, ___ na, why don't you get a job? ___ I won't give ___

Outro

Gtr. 1: w/ Rhy. Fig. 1, last 4 meas., 1 1/2 times
Gtr. 2: w/ Rhy. Fig. 2, 1 1/2 times

___ you no mon - ey; I al - ways ___ pay. ___ Na, ___ na, why don't you get a job? ___

___ Say no way, ___ say no way, ___ ya. No way. _____ Na, ___

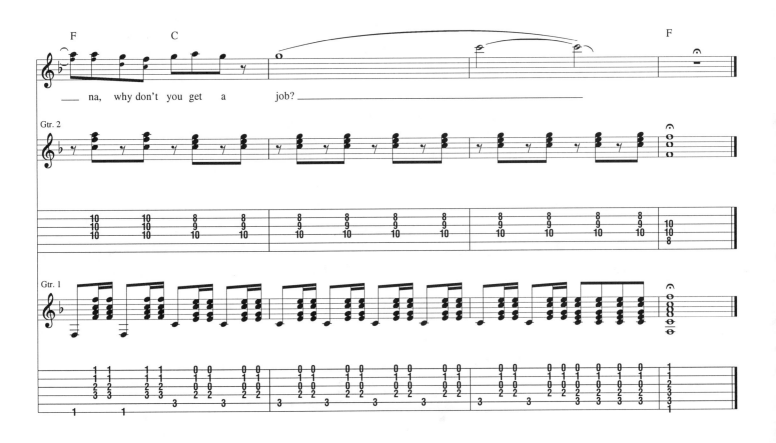

___ na, why don't you get a job? _____

Americana

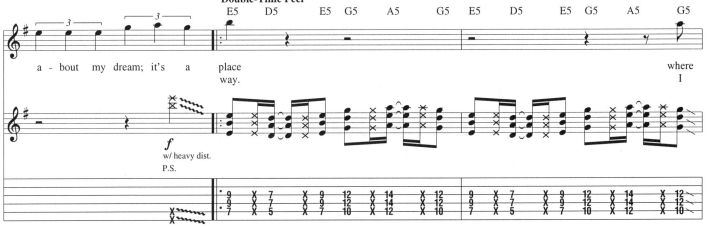

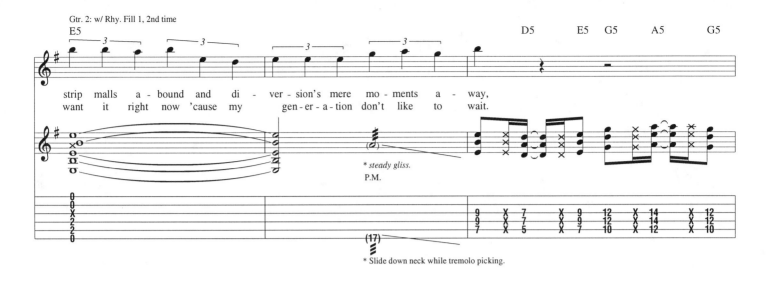

strip malls a - bound and di - ver - sion's mere mo - ments a - way,
want it right now 'cause my gen - er - a - tion don't like to wait.

* steady gliss.
P.M.

* Slide down neck while tremolo picking.

𝄋 **Pre-Chorus**

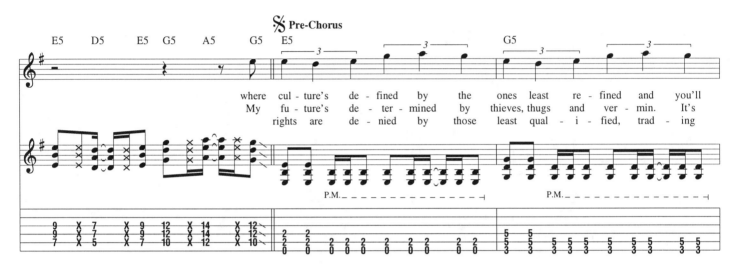

where cul - ture's de - fined by the ones least re - fined and you'll
My fu - ture's de - ter - mined by thieves, thugs and ver - min. It's
rights are de - nied by those least qual - i - fied, trad - ing

P.M. _____   P.M. _____

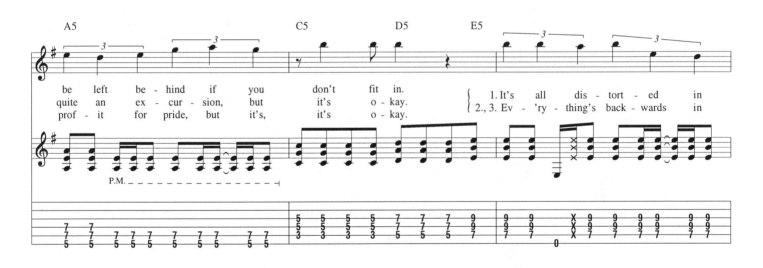

be left be - hind if you don't fit in.
quite an ex - cur - sion, but it's o - kay.
prof - it for pride, but it's, it's o - kay.

1. It's all dis - tort - ed in
2., 3. Ev - 'ry - thing's back - wards in

P.M. _____

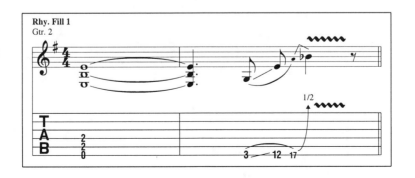

Rhy. Fill 1
Gtr. 2

1/2

Pay the Man

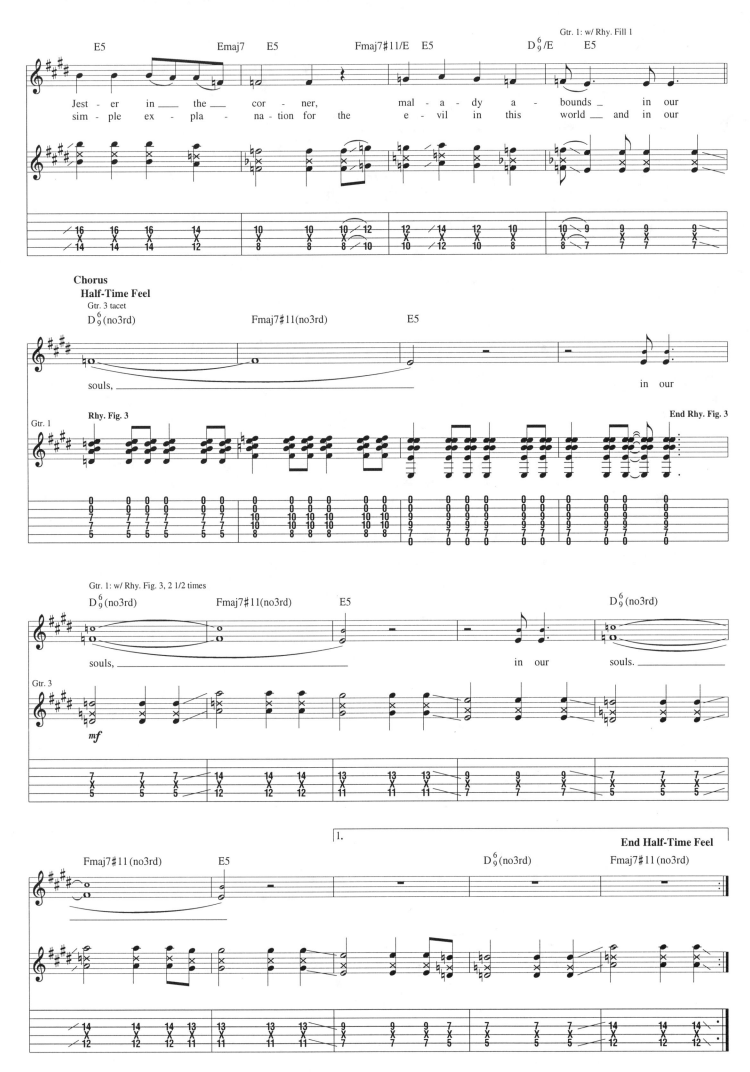

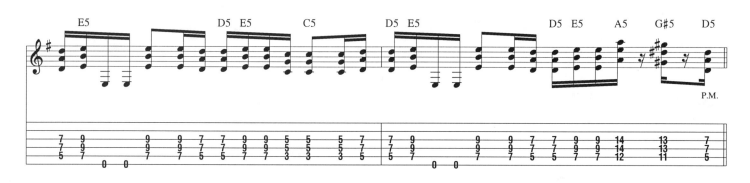

%% Verse

Gtr. 3: w/ * Rhy. Fig. 4, 4 times

1. Come down to sor - ry and sa - ble. It's al - ways the man. _ It's al - ways a - keep - ing you _ down. _
2. Look at you and your strug - gle for free - dom, but you ain't noth - ing. _ We all pay the man for liv - ing. _

* w/ P.M.

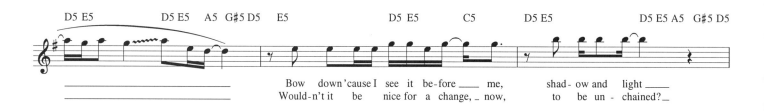

Bow down 'cause I see it be - fore _ me, shad - ow and light _
Would - n't it be nice for a change, _ now, to be un - chained? _

To Coda 1

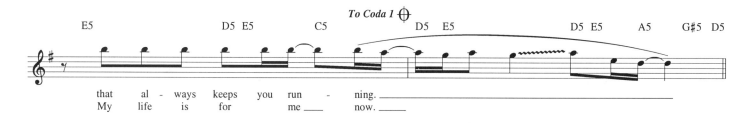

that al - ways keeps you run - ning. _
My life is for me _ now. _

%%% Chorus

Oh, oh. _ Shut up, _ you talk too much. _

Gtrs.
3 & 5 * **Rhy. Fig. 5**
(acous.)

End Rhy. Fig. 5

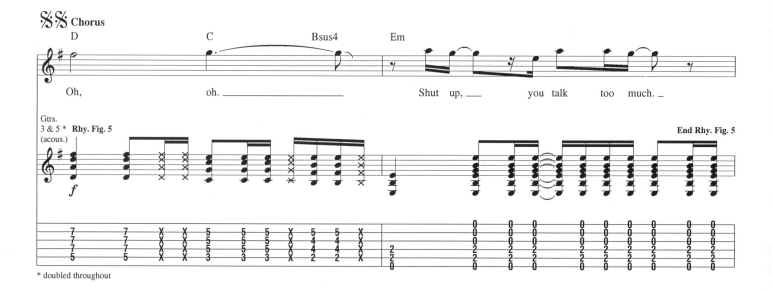

* doubled throughout

To Coda 2

Gtrs. 3 & 5: w/ Rhy. Fig. 5, 2 1/2 times

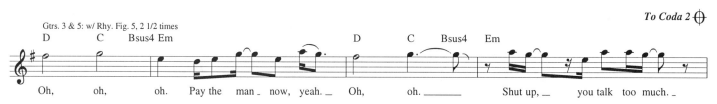

Oh, oh, oh. Pay the man _ now, yeah. _ Oh, oh. _ Shut up, _ you talk too much. _

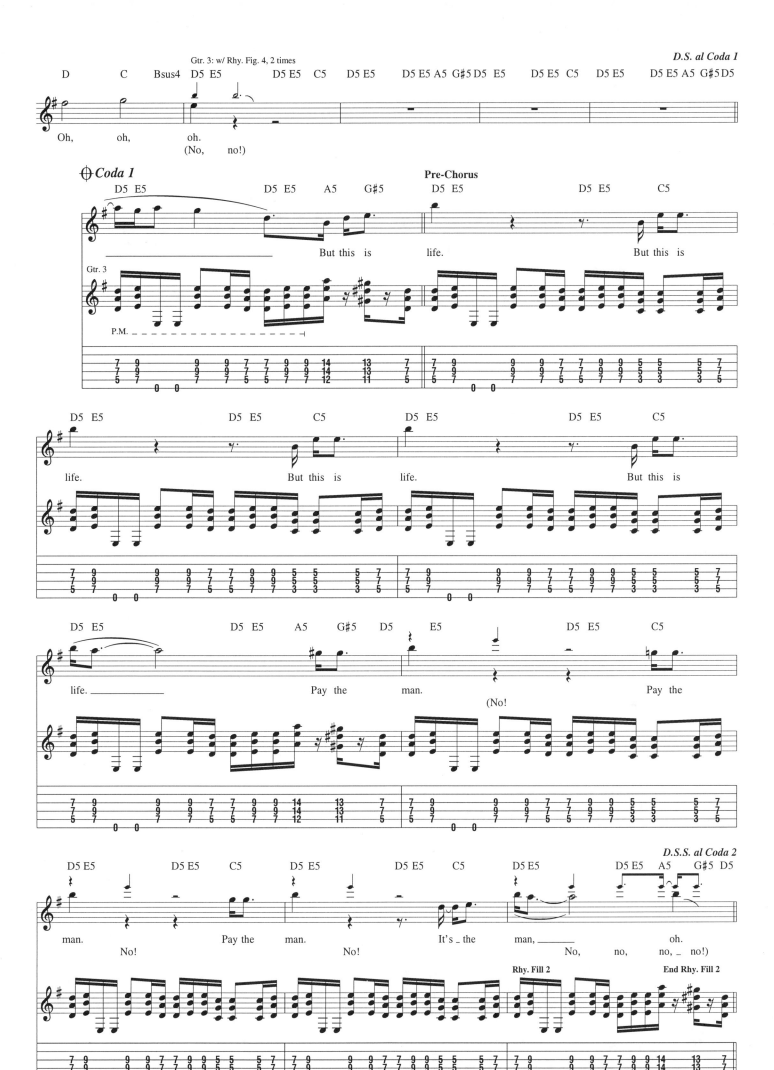

Coda 2

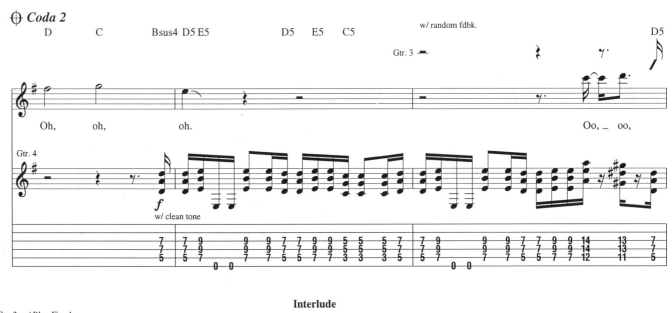

Interlude

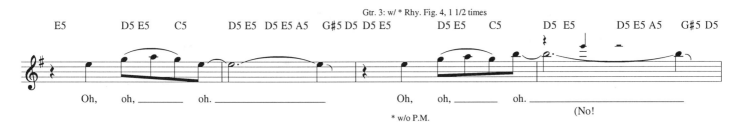

Chorus

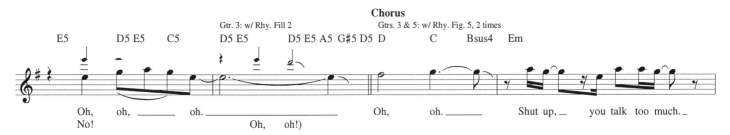

Outro

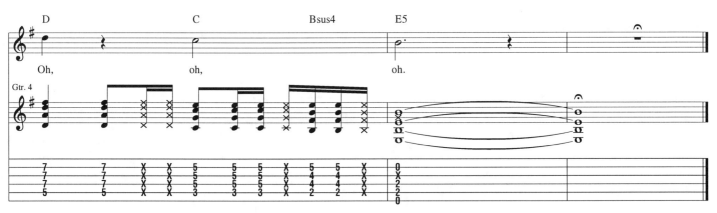

74

Guitar Notation Legend

Guitar Music can be notated three different ways: on a *musical staff*, in *tablature*, and in *rhythm slashes*.

RHYTHM SLASHES are written above the staff. Strum chords in the rhythm indicated. Use the chord diagrams found at the top of the first page of the transcription for the appropriate chord voicings. Round noteheads indicate single notes.

THE MUSICAL STAFF shows pitches and rhythms and is divided by bar lines into measures. Pitches are named after the first seven letters of the alphabet.

TABLATURE graphically represents the guitar fingerboard. Each horizontal line represents a a string, and each number represents a fret.

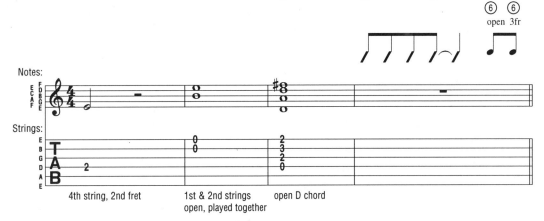

4th string, 2nd fret

1st & 2nd strings open, played together

open D chord

Definitions for Special Guitar Notation

HALF-STEP BEND: Strike the note and bend up 1/2 step.

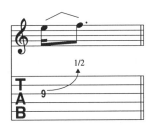

WHOLE-STEP BEND: Strike the note and bend up one step.

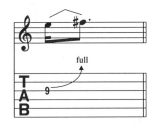

GRACE NOTE BEND: Strike the note and bend up as indicated. The first note does not take up any time.

SLIGHT (MICROTONE) BEND: Strike the note and bend up 1/4 step.

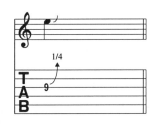

BEND AND RELEASE: Strike the note and bend up as indicated, then release back to the original note. Only the first note is struck.

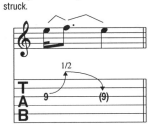

PRE-BEND: Bend the note as indicated, then strike it.

PRE-BEND AND RELEASE: Bend the note as indicated. Strike it and release the bend back to the original note.

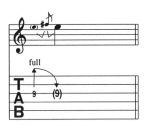

UNISON BEND: Strike the two notes simultaneously and bend the lower note up to the pitch of the higher.

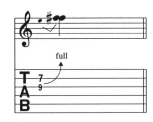

VIBRATO: The string is vibrated by rapidly bending and releasing the note with the fretting hand.

WIDE VIBRATO: The pitch is varied to a greater degree by vibrating with the fretting hand.

HAMMER-ON: Strike the first (lower) note with one finger, then sound the higher note (on the same string) with another finger by fretting it without picking.

PULL-OFF: Place both fingers on the notes to be sounded. Strike the first note and without picking, pull the finger off to sound the second (lower) note.

LEGATO SLIDE: Strike the first note and then slide the same fret-hand finger up or down to the second note. The second note is not struck.

SHIFT SLIDE: Same as legato slide, except the second note is struck.

TRILL: Very rapidly alternate between the notes indicated by continuously hammering on and pulling off.

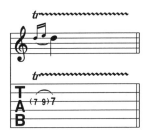

TAPPING: Hammer ("tap") the fret indicated with the pick-hand index or middle finger and pull off to the note fretted by the fret hand.

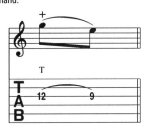

NATURAL HARMONIC: Strike the note while the fret-hand lightly touches the string directly over the fret indicated.

PINCH HARMONIC: The note is fretted normally and a harmonic is produced by adding the edge of the thumb or the tip of the index finger of the pick hand to the normal pick attack.

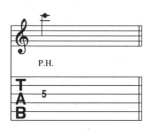

HARP HARMONIC: The note is fretted normally and a harmonic is produced by gently resting the pick hand's index finger directly above the indicated fret (in parentheses) while the pick hand's thumb or pick assists by plucking the appropriate string.

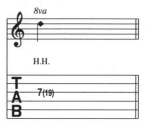

PICK SCRAPE: The edge of the pick is rubbed down (or up) the string, producing a scratchy sound.

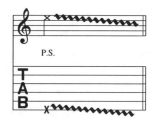

MUFFLED STRINGS: A percussive sound is produced by laying the fret hand across the string(s) without depressing, and striking them with the pick hand.

PALM MUTING: The note is partially muted by the pick hand lightly touching the string(s) just before the bridge.

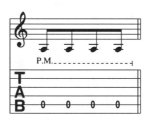

RAKE: Drag the pick across the strings indicated with a single motion.

TREMOLO PICKING: The note is picked as rapidly and continuously as possible.

ARPEGGIATE: Play the notes of the chord indicated by quickly rolling them from bottom to top.

VIBRATO BAR DIVE AND RETURN: The pitch of the note or chord is dropped a specified number of steps (in rhythm) then returned to the original pitch.

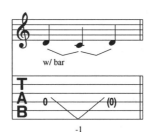

VIBRATO BAR SCOOP: Depress the bar just before striking the note, then quickly release the bar.

VIBRATO BAR DIP: Strike the note and then immediately drop a specified number of steps, then release back to the original pitch.

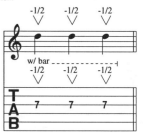

Additional Musical Definitions

 (accent) • Accentuate note (play it louder)

(accent) • Accentuate note with great intensity

(staccato) • Play the note short

⊓ • Downstroke

∨ • Upstroke

D.S. al Coda • Go back to the sign (𝄋), then play until the measure marked "**To Coda**," then skip to the section labelled "**Coda**."

D.S. al Fine • Go back to the beginning of the song and play until the measure marked "**Fine**" (end).

Rhy. Fig. • Label used to recall a recurring accompaniment pattern (usually chordal).

Riff • Label used to recall composed, melodic lines (usually single notes) which recur.

Fill • Label used to identify a brief melodic figure which is to be inserted into the arrangement.

Rhy. Fill • A chordal version of a Fill.

tacet • Instrument is silent (drops out).

• Repeat measures between signs.

 • When a repeated section has different endings, play the first ending only the first time and the second ending only the second time.

NOTE: Tablature numbers in parentheses mean:
1. The note is being sustained over a system (note in standard notation is tied), or
2. The note is sustained, but a new articulation (such as a hammer-on, pull-off, slide or vibrato begins, or
3. The note is a barely audible "ghost" note (note in standard notation is also in parentheses).